ADELE

ADELE

FIONA STERLING

CONTENTS

CHAPTER 1

Disclaimer

The content in this book is intended for informational and entertainment purposes only. While every effort has been made to ensure the accuracy of the information presented, the author and publisher make no representations or warranties of any kind, express or implied, about the completeness, accuracy, reliability, suitability, or availability with respect to the content of this book.

The views and opinions expressed in this book are those of the author and do not necessarily reflect the official policy or position of any individual, company, or organization mentioned. Any resemblance to actual persons, living or dead, or actual events is purely coincidental.

This book is not intended to defame, libel, or slander any person, company, or organization. All references to individuals, companies, products, and brands are for illustrative purposes only, and no affiliation with or endorsement by them is intended or implied.

The author and publisher disclaim any responsibility for any actions or outcomes resulting from the application of information contained in this book. Readers should seek professional advice or conduct their own research when making decisions based on the content provided.

CHAPTER 2

Introduction

Quietly influential in the transformative music of the 2010s, Adele's emotional voice resonated across the globe and spoke for a generation. Yet she herself remained largely a private person. In this essay, the presence Adele maintains—both as a professional singer and voice for the world at large—will be detailed, demonstrating the strength in the vulnerability she shares in her lyrics. This display is even prominently exemplified when she creates love songs that are multitudinous in their likenesses and sentiments, adept to reach anyone they touch. Mines of death, heartbreak, or youthful reunion, showcasing a voice that is intended for others to feel in, embodies the meaning of emotion for the many.

During the rise of the British Invasion of the 2000s, unique singers such as Amy Winehouse who boasted a deep belting voice pushed the envelop in terms of what a singer in the industry could sound or look like. Resting in the middle of the 26 million records she sold in her early years of recording was English singer Adele, who emerged as an unknown singer by the name of fourth-best for the 2008 BRIT Awards Critics' Choice competition. For at least the past two bountiful decades, few human voices have lived as presently as that of the legendary Adele. A voice as instantly recognizable in any song as it is in our homes over speakers and certainly through the shared earbuds concerning this or that heartache or joy in life, Adele's semblance is an ardent friend even in her seemly ephemeral commercial dues. Providing the world with only ten years of music, she has nonetheless touched US ears and hearts of listeners worldwide. Effects of the blue-eyed soul and popstar are innotable just by briefly examining the Englishwoman's comparably brief yet powerful list of accomplishments.

Background and Significance

In less than two decades, Adele has garnered multiple Grammy wins, headlined Glastonbury, and performed at the Oscars. With several hundred awards to her name, including Billboard's Artist of the Decade (2010s), it is clear that Adele's influence goes far beyond music. She has approved a book that explores the therapeutic nature of her songs, led to a 16% spike in pregnancy therapy inquiries (beyond referrals and word of mouth), and has produced a wealth of memes about heartbreak, apology, and confidence. Adults, Liberty, and Beyonce love and respect Adele. The Marthas, Margarets, and Roses of our world also understand what makes her tick. But how?

It is the third studio where Adele raises her association with her music to a sickeningly high level of profession. To anyone who has lost something, someone, or an identity, this album is a "map of the scars," according to Adele. Adele isn't just a singer; she's a balm. When she says "hello from the other side," we don't wonder about the songs she's sung and can't help but stare. We remember our old experiences. Given Adele's unmatched success and influence, the project's substance is both timely and important, calling for further research. The proposal's working title, Adele: The Voice of a Generation, reflects this interest and provides an indication of the distinctive content the text will generate.

CHAPTER 3

Early Life and Influences

Born in 1988 in Tottenham, London, Adele began expressing herself artistically at a very young age. She grew up listening to musicians such as the Spice Girls and Whitney Houston and started taking singing and songwriting more seriously when she was just fourteen years old. Her friends were instrumental in giving her the confidence to pursue a career in music. The more she wrote and sang, the more she began to heal emotional and mental wounds. She dealt with the difficulties of adolescence by pouring her soul into what would eventually become chart-topping singles. This contrast of real-life issues and amazing success made Adele's story unique and tapped into a relatable part of human nature, which is why it resonated so deeply with the millions of people who purchased her three albums.

As Adele pursued her career, she was influenced by the artistic talents of her English and Irish family. Her mother's stage fright, grandfather's obsession with jukeboxes, and familial rejection of privacy made Adele eager to share her experiences and musical perspective with the world. Many artists create based on what they know, and in this case, she simply knew her family. Growing up listening to Etta James, Ella Fitzgerald, and influential American country music shaped Adele's voice and the styles she would capitalize on as an adult. Adele's idols also include Mary J. Blige, Jill Scott, and Lauryn Hill, who are known for blending R&B, hip-hop, and neo-soul, much like Adele tried with her sophomore album, 21. The emotional prowess of these singers, however, is what most captivated Adele and prepared her for her rise, as she notes, "I just found that when I discovered - you know, like Lauryn and Mary J. Blige and stuff - I just found a big connection between my struggles and the themes in the R&B music I was listening to."

Childhood in London

Adele—now among the most renowned singers worldwide—is known for her mature sound and universal lyricism. Her music has gained her a massive international following and eight Grammy Awards, as she has conquered the charts with her popular albums. This pioneering lady, strong soloist, and songwriter is cheerfully cheered by all of her listeners.

Adele's birth name is Adele Laurie Blue Adkins. She was born in North London on May 5th, 1988, with her mother, Penny Adkins, essentially raising her on her own. She has a cousin with whom she was quite close when she was little.

Adele is persuaded to aspire for a livelihood in music. Her childhood had a major influence on her as a result of this. She grew in a region with a rich musical landscape and a large variety of music. This influenced her deeply, causing her to pursue music as a profession. Adolescents totally followed her newly discovered net heroine at the BRIT School! The Brit School for Performing Arts and Technology currently has a programme for young prodigies in the fields of music and dance. The West Norwood spot friends, including singer Jessie J, initially grew up in South London. She then went to High School in Essex, before moving to Tottenham in North London. The "Chasing Pavements" crooner has become close friends with 16-year-old Dylan Newman after meeting him at Kings College, London in May. Adele, who alerted him, told him to "keep his eyes on the prize!"

CHAPTER 4

Musical Beginnings

As a new artist just a short time ago, Adele's musical journey is a collection of her early hands-on training and lessons in heartache that have been masterfully expressed in her various songs. She's sung in class shows where her renditions were only mediocre, predominantly by her own estimation. As the years went by, she continued to sing, though music was more of a passion for her than anything else during this particular era of her life. The young lady has been a student singer at "music" oriented schools as well as a student singer at "sympathetic" educational institutions, as an example.

She also began singing, playing the guitar, drumming, keyboarding, and putting pen to paper in songwriting during her high school years. This was a time in her life when music accomplished two vital things for her. During this phase of her life, it was an outlet that enabled her to be free from the negative feelings and experiences she was going through at the time. Adele was taught to play her mom's guitar at the age of twelve by a certain substitute educator when she had enrolled in her first class of guitar that year. This particular lesson didn't seem to mean much at the time to the young student, since Adele only took his advice slightly, albeit this one time. Just two or three increasingly frustrating times later when teaching herself how to play the guitar without the assistance of written guidance or any human instruction, Adele was reminded of the advice she'd received from this certain teacher, and it dawned on her right then and there as to how essential it was to take his advice at his word and start learning the guitar from square one almost.

Demo Recordings

One month before she was signed to XL Recordings, Adele graduated from BRIT School in Croydon. She had eight or nine demo recordings when Richard Russell visited her home. Rick Rubin and many other record producers wanted to work with her, but Russell enjoyed her music. In 2021, The Observer wrote, without difficulty, that an eleven-year-old could hear the talent in Adele's recordings for XL Recordings. These tracks were sent to the A&R department at the Beggars Group, and two weeks later Adele had the personnel of The Fader agonized as they recorded her for a feature.

The demo collection on her MySpace was retweeted and shared by more people than any other artist. These recordings were the ones that helped the fledgling artist decide to make music for her life. This album was supposed to be recorded by Aaron Ipson just before and while she was at Cava Studios in Glasgow. Although she was working at the studio, she spent more time at work there than she did on the record. Adele had just recorded her eleventh song, the sixteenth take was written in April, and she and Ipson then had some songs to choose from. The recording was supposed to start shortly and Ipson was supposed to be there until the end of June to complete it. A four-page article detailed the life of the star, how she was discovered by Richard Russell of XL, and debated whether or not she would have the "fourth emergency service for an industry in trouble".

CHAPTER 5

Breakthrough Success

It takes a rare artist to gain global recognition on the power of her voice and songwriting skill alone, without the common added perk of flashy visuals to back it up, but Adele can do just that. Although she signed a record deal at just 18 years old, the British singer's career really began to take off when she released her debut album, 19, in 2008. With her loose, bluesy pop influenced by Wanda Jackson, Mary J. Blige, and Peggy Lee, she found international success by positioning herself as a worthy heir to such grand old tradition of powerful, independent women. Two years of inspiration and creative energy resulted in the record-shattering success of her sophomore album, 21. Both the album and its lead-off single, "Rolling in the Deep," established Adele as a unique talent in the modern era.

Adele spent the vast majority of her childhood in London, where she attended the BRIT School for Performing Arts and Technology. In addition to her academic studies, she also received a decent amount of musical training. Her career in the music industry began when she was approached by an A&R scout who asked the young singer if she was interested in pursuing a recording contract. The offer would eventually lead to her signing a contract with XL Recordings (partially due to the audible jubilation of company executives when they finally heard her sing). Hitting the scene in 2007, she soon earned the number two position in the BBC "Sound of 2008" poll and also received the 2008 Critics' Choice prize at the Brit Awards. The following year, Adele released her first album, 19. It entered the British charts at the number one position.

Debut Album: 19

In terms of music, Adele sang at the concert "Foundation" in Lodz, the "O2 Academy", "Nightjar" or "The BodyGuard" in London and Birmingham. She was also a soloist of the RTV Slovakia Symphony Orchestra and a member of the vocal group "Pro Cantores". At the same time, the singer was involved in events of local significance, such as the 25th anniversary celebration of the film for which Poland received the first Oscar in history ("Those Amakatu") of Lodz's monuments for the day, etc. During the A-level period, Adele travelled around Europe with a group of young Irish composers and Chamber musicians (Chamber Orchestra of Europe and Marino College). The concerts took place in Paris, Dublin and in two most beautiful concert halls in Berlin. In October 2016, she also had a childhood dream – the premiere of an album with film compositions "MOJE TANGO". The premiere took place at the IFF Falenica.

'Sweetest Devotion' was the name of the first harmony on Adele's sleeve. A singer born in the district of Tottenham, London, was born on May 5, 1988, after a break of several weeks. "19" was the album that the audience really learned about her as a mature singer, even if she was a teenager at that time. Adele then spoke the iconic phrase, "This album is to represent the 19-year-old girls, and I believe it will be able to break this kind." On December 19, 2007, with the help of Jonathan Dikon, September was released as the first single with this amazing set. Like the immortal "Chasing Pavements", she came out earlier than the record she came from. The player entered the official UK singles chart at number 7. On December 1, 2007, the young character announced that "Chasing Pavements" would be released as the only premiere piece in the UK. Produced by British artist Eg White, Chasing Pavements became a chart-topping single, performing well in sales and radio airplay. In 2009, Adele joined Coldplay for eight concerts of their Hyundai Card Super Concert 19 tour. These concerts took place in Seoul, South Korea in April 2017.

CHAPTER 6

Artistry and Style

Vocal Talent Adele's vocal talent drew the attention of the entire world. Her soulful voice belts through songs like Someone Like You and Hello. The multiple Grammy award-winning singer is known for her deeply emotional lyrics, and she often combines delicate piano music as part of her signature sound. Some describe Adele's style as pop-soul. She combines elements of classic songs with a modern twist that many love. Classically trained, Adele's vocal prowess and powerful voice come across in all of her music.

Expressive Adele is a truly expressive singer. Many believe that her artistry is one of the more clear reasons that she has appealed to the masses. In her music, Adele often talks about themes that everyone can relate to, like heartache, love, and hope. However, she does so in a way that is graceful and truthful. When she describes the lyrics of her songs, she claims that she is telling the story of her own life. She writes music as a way of healing. Adele has also stated that she enjoys "writing music that is completely out of her control." It is a way for her to be lucid.

Sofia Battle, writer for the blog "Even While I'm Awake," calls Adele's music haunting. This is true for many. Adele's style, voice, truthfulness in her lyrics, and general flair for the music world are beyond that of a mere pop singer. In an "Extra" interview, Adele confesses, "I'd never see music as a competition between artists. I don't put the music out as a competition, even from when I was in school." Instead, she produces music as a way of combing through trying life experiences and expressing the facets of life that others may miss.

Vocal Range and Technique

Adele comes from the large tradition of British women singers that also includes Dusty Springfield, Annie Lennox, and Amy Winehouse. As such, she carries that heritage into the twenty-first century, in part because her voice is such a singular one. She is a full-figured woman with a full voice, a voice that conveys emotion and carries gracefully into the upper reaches of the alto range and beyond. Being a pop singer, Adele could, in theory, produce a sound that is more smooth and light, but that just is not her natural voice. Her shout can be harsh, which has been noted often in commentary. However, it gives her sound a sense of urgency and makes the singer who can summon it seem like a person inevitable.

From a technical perspective, we could note that to make a sound as full and deep as hers, she has to have very strong, properly functioning chest voice that she can continue to use as she ascends in pitch, and her belting technique needs to be worked out to avoid damage. On a musical level, her ability to control and shape the sound allows her to create a deep sense of pathos. When delivered through this unique acoustic, Adele's smoky sound and her words take on an authenticity that allows listeners to develop a strong identification with the song's sentiment. The story that Adele's voice shape-tells about Adele as a person is the next issue to be broached.

CHAPTER 7

Impact and Legacy

In her body of work, Adele has woven together universal human experiences into a soulful tapestry that continues to captivate legions of fans across the globe. Widely recognized for her emotive delivery and versatility, Adele has also helped make mainstream music a site that contains cultural critique and introspection. Adele's impact on the music landscape is immense and her influence extends to artists like Lady Gaga, Beyoncé, and Ed Sheeran who have all publicly named her as an inspiration. Though TIME dubbed 50-year-old Michael Jackson the 'Artist of the Decade' for the 1980s, many music scholars expect thirty-three-year-old Adele to receive the title in the United States for the 2010s. Furthermore, her iconic single, "Someone Like You," a Rebound Song that "helped the newly single write about their own past relationships and gain closure," ended up becoming "the 'coronation' of the Upfront Facebook Ritual."

Adele's music also prompted discussions of self-disclosure in culture and the hyper-individuated 'Facebook Self' era; just as Adele shares the most vulnerable and honest aspects of her personal life with her listeners, so too do many Facebook users display intimate thoughts and images to the world on their networked newsfeeds. In 2011, Rolling Stone, Pitchfork, and Time magazine all named 21 the best album of the year, VH1 declared Adele the 'The Greatest Diva of 21st Century,' Essence named her the 2011 Breakthrough Artist of the Year, Billboard named "Rolling in the Deep" their #1 'Song of the Year,' and Barbara Streisand introduced Adele's performance of "Someone Like You" on the 2011 VMAs with a short message, "This is Adele and she is simply special. What a talent. Two years ago she released her second album '21' and her voice is always ringing in my head." In "2011's Year in Pop Culture"—an infographic published on TV Guide's website—Adele was honored for her "Top-Selling Album." Her name appeared alongside Adele's picture along with the text "'21'—4 million copies (to date)." Adele's most recent album, "30," released in 2021, adds complexity and range to her public persona in ways that address the current social issues of today. The musical compositions that Adele layers with text ask important questions about identity and change, and add to the discourse of self-authority in culture. If her first album was a "breakup album" reflecting on love and lack, and her second album was a rebound album that helped her and her listeners gain closure, then her third album poetically explores a more interior melodrama along with issues of renewal, motherhood, and adulting. Adele's modern public image is multifaceted and works to reveal what society believes about the nature of change and identity. In addressing the topics of motherhood, love, and change within her dense lyric and melodic compositions, Adele reveals what anyone going through a breakup, a personal transformation, or a mid-life crisis would say about the changes in identity that Lagrange theorizes.

Cultural Influence

Adele has established herself as one of the 21st century's strongest pop and soul voices. Her durability in the music world has further proved her to be a transcendent legend in all senses, with her aptly titled 30 being an amalgamation of a days-of-yore lounge band aesthetic and contemporary pop sensibilities. With ten years of proven results, it is safe to say that Adele is more of a counseling service than an artist, with her most famous work coming in the form of the smash album 21 that had the entirety of the aughts baby populace diving into a bowl of ice cream. Adele's subsequent work has positioned the artist as the poster child for therapeutic excellence, with subsequent records 25 and 30 each carrying the torch for comfort around the world.

Adele has made a definite impact on the music industry since her arrival on the scene. Indeed, her eclectic blend of soulful pop ballads, captivating lyrics, and astonishing voice whenever she sings has earned the British chanteuse numerous Billboard Hot 100 hits, praise from critics and fans alike, and an astounding collection of accolades to boot. The cultural impact of Adele has been significant, with her emotive lyrics and anthems being identified as "hugely popular" by academic sources. The prevalent theme in much of Adele's work is around love, betrayal, loss, and family, which extends into broader societal and familial expectations of marriage, gender roles, and relationships, and the shared sorrows and struggles of womanhood in particular. Her music has also been described as "powerful," part of a broader trend in the 2010s of pop music about triumph, empowerment, and sorrow that "captured the feeling of a tumultuous and perilous post-recession society." Like the artists of the '60s and '70s, Adele took raw emotion and utilized orchestral and "grandiose" songwriting to reflect on elements of society that might otherwise be exposed in a folk song.

CHAPTER 8

Personal Life and Public Image

Adele married her long-term boyfriend, Simon Konecki, in 2016, although the couple divorced in 2019. They have a son, Angelo, who was born in 2012. Adele has been emphasized in the media as one of pop music's most iconic singers and female vocalists and has been various compared to American singers like Whitney Houston and Fiona Apple, describing her as an arts-defining, multi-faceted artist. Adele's personality has been called down-to-earth and massively likable. Adele can be seen as a contradictory figure within the public eye: while being a working-class woman from the inner city, well-suited to the average Briton, she is also fantastically wealthy which differentiates her from her fan base. Her favorite artist, Ella Fitzgerald, Adele did name her dog after an icon, calling the creatures a "cleaner, happier Carter."

An admitted lover of the drink and regularly speaking openly about her drinking habits, Adele has also made rounds for reshaping her body, dropping from a size 16 to a size 8 in 2012. However, she outright has attacked speculation in the media about her body and believes that tabloids are insulting smaller people as well as plus-sized people as a result of attacking her for her monastic weight loss and assuming that it can have only been motivated by her desire to fit in. She has also objected to her boyfriend and husband, Simon, being labeled as 'unattractive' by the media, pointing out the toxicity of telling men that they must be conventionally 'handsome' and actors who 'look good' in order to be considered as successful or happy. Uniform circular motion.

Relationships and Family

At the age of 10, Adele moved with her mother and relied extensively on public transportation, as she did not have a driver's license. In September 2011, the British magazine The Sunday Times reported that Adele and Konecki had been dating since January 2012. The couple had a son, Angelo, on 19 October 2012. In 2016, Adele confirmed her marriage to Konecki; she had been married since 2016 but given her desire for privacy had chosen not to make it public. In April 2019, it emerged that the pair had separated. Some of Adele's early lovers inspired her first two albums, 19 and 21.

Adele has two half-brothers from her father's previous marriage. Her relationship with him deteriorated, and she moved in with friends instead. According to Adele, it was her mother who worked and came to school to get her. Her mother also helped tell the story of the song "Hometown Glory". In her 2015 Time 100 entry, Bette Midler wrote, "Her music is the voice of every underpaid and overworked parent, every bereft lover, every bludgeoned spirit who has lost all hope. She's our champion." In a review of 21, the American magazine Rolling Stone labeled her "the voice of Nile Rodgers," publicly apologized and asked for a new face. While being interviewed for a more recent remix of her song Hello by Lionel Richie, Adele said, "I take off when I'm done." She left the show after 19 or 21 and listened to a lot of jazz and seminal manner. "I wanted to write like him or Paris."

CHAPTER 9

Global Recognition and Awards

A dele has found success and recognition on a global scale. Her music has resonated with people across generations and countries, all of whom try to echo her distinctive voice. In 2011, VH1 announced that the United States had incorporated Adele into the list of influential artists of this century. According to Spotify, "Someone Like You" by Adele is one of the most popular songs played at weddings around the world. Through her voice, she has given a voice to people from around the world, surpassed borders and languages, and garnered deserving appreciation and praise. Her personality and voice have molded her into an international personality, impacting millions of people around the world.

Given not only Adele's vocal prowess but also the depth of her lyricism, it should come as no surprise that she has scooped up multiple awards since her debut in the music industry. Over the course of her career, she has won 15 Grammy Awards. This includes accolades for Best New Artist, Album of the Year, Record of the Year, and Song of the Year. Across the UK and Europe, Adele has also taken home numerous awards. She's won BRIT awards, Urban Music Awards, NME Awards, MTV Europe Awards, and more. The global impact of her universally loved music has been reflected in some of the world's highest honors. She has won the Grammy award 18 times. She was also included in the prestigious TIME 100 list for 2011 and 2012 and was honored with an MBE in 2013 for her services to music.

Grammy Awards
Adele: One of 21st Century Soul Stars
The British singer Adele has been awarded the Grammy Awards twelve times. This is a very impressive result for one of the most talented vocalists of the 21st century. She is one of the representatives of the neo-soul direction. Like John Legend, Alicia Keys, and Jill Scott, she uses soul music as a basis, but with modern pop and contemporary R&B sound. Her deep and hoarse voice brought her the title of the "voice of a generation", as well as the title "American music anal artist" (she is a Briton). She released four albums: "19" (the age of Adele during the recording sessions), "21", "25", and "30".

From an early age, Adele had a great love for music. Her favorite singers were the Spice Girls and Pink. She wrote her first song when she was 15, and as a teenager, she was awarded Britain's most important national music award, the Brit Awards Critics' Awards. She graduated from the BRIT School for Performing Arts & Technology, the starting platform of Amy Winehouse, Leona Lewis, and Kate Nash. "19" (the album was released on January 28, 2008) was a good success, but it was not until the next album that Adele became known in the United States. The young woman's life has changed beyond recognition, something she never thought she would experience. "I am very proud of my success and happy with all this attention," she says herself. "But it is the music that counts in the first place." She received six Grammy Awards (the world's leading music prize) for "21". This award is awarded annually in Los Angeles.

Adele had big competition during the "Grammys", including Lady Gaga and Bruno Mars, but it was she who appeared on stage as a laureate several times.

CHAPTER 10

Evolution of Sound

From starting off her journeys with heartbreak anthems such as "Someone Like You" to belting out feel-good bangers like "Send My Love" off of her much-awaited third studio album "25," Adele's sound (and her styling!) has evolved remarkably over the years. In fact, if you listen carefully, you can pretty much track not just her music but the major milestones in Adele's life through her albums. As she gears up to release her new body of work, we take a look at what has been, and what's set to come.

"19" (2008) Influenced by the blues, jazz, and soul, Adele's debut album, 19, was released when she was, in fact, 19. The album won her her first Grammy and a growing fan base thanks to the big hits on the album like "Chasing Pavements," "Hometown Glory," and "Make You Feel My Love."

"21" (2011) Her sophomore album, 21, was formed entirely around a break-up gone wrong. Written with themes of causing heartbreak, having a heart full of anger, and an album full of tear-jerker lines, Adele's R&B influenced pop songs have windows-down-weeping-on-long-drives capabilities. The album proved to be an instant hit, and according to NME, it is one of the Top 500 Greatest Albums of All Time.

"25" (2015) Influenced by the old-fashioned tunes from the 1920s, 25 marked a shift for Adele. Nearly all the tunes on the album are much happier; it was called a "make up album" by Adele herself. The style of music also saw a shift as it moved into the genre of pop. Songs such as "Water Under The Bridge," "I Miss You," and "When We Were Young" really rocked Adele's record as they weren't just about loose stories, but about wanting those feelings back and missing that age that you will never be able to describe, physically.

Shifts in Musical Style

In discussing her music, most critics point out that Adele has shifted her styling a little bit in each record she has made. 19, for instance, was made before she was famous, during late nights spent in a small studio on the weekends. Many have said she was heavily influenced by Bob Dylan and Norah Jones. 21, made right after she skyrocketed to fame, has more of a modern, mainstream sound with a bit more pop mixed in, although most will admit that it's not actually her writing, but everything else about the album, that makes it what it is. 25 continued to develop her unique style, although many say she became more focused on the effect of her album and less on improving her songwriting. What parts of her style developed in her music? Did she develop in 'craving permanence' or revolutionism, or in creating a voice that she has played from day one in order to be as popular and cherished and listened to by fans, rather than cookies to make her writing trendy? Well, specifically, a lot about Adele's style has changed from her singles to her albums themselves. Throughout it all, she managed to go from being influenced by Norah Jones to being a part of the reason that albums of the 'big-voiced female apartment singer' archetype can be commercially successful even without the pop element. Again, this is just one aspect of her style or career, but in discussing her music we have kept all of these origins in mind.

Initially, her style shifted just as anyone else's does: as she progressed as a singer/songwriter, her style would progress with her. For instance, when she penned her first two majorly popular singles - "Hometown Glory" and "Chasing Pavements" - Parsons is pretty sure she didn't sit down with a hit-bound checklist consisting of introductory verses, a catchy chorus, musical "climaxes," and various hooks or earworms. However, when Saunders saw Adele live three years after she released 19, his report seemed more concrete. He was impressed with her voice, but described her very jazz/R&B-heavy performance as not having any big high points. For whatever the reason, in the few years between her debut and the making of her sophomore album, Adele softened her jazz influences, embraced pop, and replaced X. Matt Sayles attributes some of this revolution to the fact that "she wanted to be able to sing her own lyrics to new people." According to Adele herself, 21 was made using 'an odd mixture of [Mumford and Sons and Rilo Kiley, plus just tiny bits of Jay Z]' as an influence or inspiration. In any case, by 21, more musical and songwriting elements began to be viewed by Adele critics as decidedly her.

CHAPTER 11

Collaborations and Duets

Adele has released a number of songs and albums either as collaborations (that is, a partnership between two or more artists, sometimes from different genres) or as duets (where the song only features two voices). Something that all these songs and albums have in common is that the featured artists are part of the credits – meaning they contributed lyrics, musical elements, or production to the final product.

Adele's featured artists include established musicians such as the likes of Jack Peñate, her "cousin" (note: she doesn't have siblings), and even Santana featuring Steven Tyler. In the other extreme of guestlist is her friend Lloyd and unknown and/or low-key artists like, for instance, J. Williams. When she was a teenager and in the early stages of her career, Adele participated in a few cover songs, mostly from bands/singers that she admires and has some inspiration in her music. The number of cover songs that Adele did at the time are roughly 30, most of them when she used to perform at the Stage Door pub. Here are a few collaborations and duets in which Adele has featured: "Hometown Glory," "That's It, I Quit, I'm Movin' On," "Natural Woman," "Steady My Heart (Part 1)," "Kissing You," "S9 Music Freestyle," "This Is Who I Am," "Cry Me a River," and "Someone Like You."

Some of Adele's songs are not in her albums, one way or another. Some are songs featuring other artists, others might be alternative versions of her songs. "Many Shades of Black" features The Raconteurs, a blues rock band formed in the city of Detroit, US, in 2005. The group is composed of Jack White (guitars and vocals), Mark Watrous (second guitar and Shaker), Dean Fertita (bass and keys), and Patrick Keeler (drums). Produced and released by The Raconteurs, it was distributed by Warner Bros, the label which Adele was launched in the US. The song is number 13 on their second album "Consolers of the Lonely," which came out on March 25, 2008. Although Adele was without an international record contract at that time, the song was successful and managed to sell worldwide and be charted in several countries. On March 30, 2008, the single peaked at number 50 on the US Modern Rock Tracks, remaining for 17 weeks on the chart. Following this trend, "Many Shades of Black" took first place on the Japan Hot 100, for the week ending October 3, 2008. Allen Hughes has recorded a music video for the song, in which Adele, Jack White, and Patrick Keeler appeared. A duet with American pop punk band Paramore was recorded for their 5th studio album "After Laughter," which was released on May 12, 2017. The song also features American singer-songwriter Joe Jonas.

Notable Partnerships

In addition to extensive praise from critics in the music industry, Adele has attracted attention from a global audience by working with other well-known artists. These partnerships come in all shapes and sizes, but it is these duets and collaborations that have provided the singer with opportunities to continue introducing her music to people all over the world. It resumed in 2008 with the re-promotion of "Make You Feel My Love". Periodically, Adele and Sam Smith face claims of a rivalry or feud due to their similar career paths: both are British, and both became mainstream artists in soul pop in the 21st century, achieving extreme success worldwide. In 2008, Adele and The Raconteurs released a split single on 7-inch vinyl for Record Store Day to raise money for charity. The Raconteurs performed their version of 'Many Shades of Black', and Adele covered their song 'Steady, As She Goes'.

The band has since been a notable exception. Adele wrote three songs on the album 21, including the international hits "Turning Tables" and "One and Only". On March 5, 2011, Adele performed "Rolling in the Deep" with Jennifer Nettles on a television special CMT Crossroads. The episode also included behind-the-scenes footage of the making of the special, as well as the pairing's respective previous hits. Nettles, who was then pregnant with her first child, joked that she and Adele would start a band and Adele would carry a baby for her. In September 2011, Adele released the song "Someone like You", co-written with Dan Wilson, from the band Semisonic. The song topped the chart in the UK, with Adele reading out a message the pair received via Twitter from a nurse in England. The song also reached No. 2 in the US; Wilson later wrote on his blog: "The song hit the radio, Adele performed it at the Brit Awards. The Band Perry arranged a live performance."

CHAPTER 12

Philanthropy and Social Causes

Adele has been open about her support for over 40 charitable causes. Her philanthropy has largely remained under the radar, with donations made to institutions such as London's Hometown Raise, United Way Worldwide, and Partners of Health Sierra Leone fund earning her high praise. Adele is enthusiastic about using her platform to draw attention to a variety of social causes.

Some of her acts of philanthropy are unbeknownst to the public. In 2016 at the British Summer Carnival, Adele hosted a private screening for the survivors of the Grenfell Tower inferno, albeit not publicizing the event. She also paid for the flight and accommodation of her friend, who has genes for rare litter spacing disorder Brittle Corset Syndrome, to visit her from Nigeria to England. The singer celebrated her 33rd birthday with a photoshopped image of herself in a low-cut black suit in front of a fountain. In the previous year, she had requested donations from friends, family, and fans for the Grenfell Phoenix Ark, but revealed that she wasn't able to partake in the auction. After a stained glass window honoring the youngest Grenfell Tower victim was commissioned, Adele is said to have declared, "We must look after and help our community".

Support for Various Charities

Known for her gargantuan voice and colossal talent, bolstered by her prolific songwriting capabilities, Adele is one of the premier talents to have emerged in the past decade. Nevertheless, her talents are not restricted to her vocals and her songwriting - she is known as a person who is not only gifted artistically but also as a person whose kind-heartedness knows no boundaries. Her large philanthropy and support for different causes are another avenue to understand her better.

In recent years, Adele has raised money for several notable causes. Many of her fan bases consider it their mission to help the less fortunate, thanks to her individual capacity to draw attention. From causes that affect her such as heart disease and cancer to broader problems like healthcare, Adele gives attention to myriad causes. Throughout her life, her art has always been deeply enmeshed with her truth. If her art couldn't reflect her advocacy, supporting these causes is how she can live her truth. This Real Love message reveals the simple but profound idea that beating cancer (or any illness or other life-threatening situations) happens when love, empathy, and support are shared among the community.

Music artist Adele has chosen a variety of charitable organizations, including children's hospitals and healthcare aid organizations to benefit from her largesse. She's donated proceeds to different causes, ranging from profound otherness to HIV/AIDS, as well as to provide lupus and cancer therapy for children. Adele made a considerable contribution to Caudwell Children in 2021 that made headlines when the news came out. The "Hello" composer donated £380,000 to provide children with top-of-the-line audiology care. "We are amazed by your unbelievable work," said the star. Adele took to her official Instagram page to tell followers she is selling her new t-shirts as part of the charity effort, and she followed the announcement with another in support of the organization. In a T-shirt sleeve email, the "Set Fire to the Rain" singer told people she worked with on Instagram's Business account. "It's taken a tremendous amount of effort to make this little thing come to pass, and I am truly thankful for all their help."

CHAPTER 13

Challenges and Resilience

Inspired by a concert she attended, Samson wrote "Daydreamer," a song that changed her life by getting her a record deal with XL, not to mention the attention of both fans and critics alike. Remarkably, "Daydreamer" also brought out Adele's heart and ambition. She managed all this by being candid and open, two qualities that informed the content of nearly all the other songs on her debut album, 19. On tracks like "Chasing Pavements" and "Hometown Glory," she sang about her emotions and experiences in a voice that could boom like a thunderstorm or whisper like a soft rain. Critics praised her "sly, attractive voice," said she "knows when to lay back," and marveled over how utterly "her heartaches resonate."

While Adele's voice and maturity were remarkable, her path to stardom has not always been easy, even if the struggles painted her talent in sharp relief. Disillusioned by the music industry after her record label merged with another company, and short on funds after a long tour in the United States, she released a collection of tracks and videos on MySpace in hopes of getting the album to influential people. Three years after being taken on by XL, she was dropped by the label because of a change in leadership. She was broke and threw up for days after getting dropped by the label. That same year, she held down a pair of low-paying jobs because the government gave her just £30 a week, even though her rent was £400. Determined to find a way to exploit her talents to their fullest, she worked as a babysitter, a shop clerk, and a receptionist at a salon and put her career on the backburner while she built up her finances. The budding star paid her band members in food, taking them out to dinner and to an open-mic night at which they performed while they were living in a flat in London. It was while living here that she wrote some of the songs on her debut album. Despite the challenges Adele has faced, she has managed to land herself at least two of the most successful record deals any artist could achieve.

Struggles with Fame

Celebrities are regular people, but their lives can be more complicated because of their fame. Similarly, as the daughter of a single mom who barely supported herself, Adele's focus was never on money or fame. She just loved to sing. Other people, however, knew she was bound for success. Since releasing her first album, 19, in 2007, Adele has become a celebrity, not only known for her incredibly powerful, soulful voice, but also for her struggles. In this chapter and the next, we'll look at some specific struggles she has faced. The first struggle we're going to look at is related to her fame.

In 2011, just after the release of the album 21, Adele was an international success. She was doing what she absolutely loved, but the pressures were immense because of it. She would later say, "I wasn't a famous person. I was a famous singer." For this reason, Adele felt that she hadn't signed up for the craziness that was her life. As a worldwide phenomenon, she was constantly on tour around the world and mastered the art of traveling, but found it to be "humongous pressure." On top of that, Adele was still young, in her early 20s, and had trouble dealing with her emotions and the responsibilities of a young adult. Later that year, she had to cancel two sold-out tours in the United States and, in fact, underwent surgery to remove her vocal cord haemorrhage.

CHAPTER 14

Film and Television Ventures

Since the release of 21, Adele has found herself in demand in the film and television industry. Adele contributed the song "Skyfall," used in the 2012 James Bond film of the same name, which she and Paul Epworth co-wrote and composed. The song quickly became a big hit in the United Kingdom and is often regarded as one of the greatest James Bond themes of all time. It won the Academy Award, Golden Globe, and Brit Award for Best Original Song. She expertly melds the film's title with allusions to its lyrics in the same way that she often bridges emotions with her musical content.

Frequent collaborator and "Send My Love" co-writer Greg Kurstin returned as executive producer, partnered with the likes of Max Martin, Billie Eilish and Finneas, and Inflo for an album that combines past and future – emotion and experimentation – saved and sacrificed, but in a completely different way than 25.

The album uses mainly R&B elements to great success, demonstrating Adele's unmatched vocal range and believability. Where the power of the songs on 25 came from her ability to connect with and interpret them in a uniquely individual way, the lyrics of 30 are more global and relatable. Adele also collaborates with other songwriters this time around including MNEK, Tobias Jesso Jr, Diane Warren and Jamie Scott to bring both collaborations and co-writing back in her fold.

Half Time (2023)

In late November 2022, it was announced that Adele would be making her acting debut in Half Time – director Zack Snyder's rise-and-fall biopic about disgraced basketball referee Tim Donaghy. The film is set to star Ethan Hawke and Daveed Diggs. In Half Time, Adele reportedly has a supporting role as "a suburban mom." There is currently no release date for the film.

Soundtrack Contributions

Certainly, Adele's vocal contributions didn't cause the soundtrack trend, but she has added a robust stamp to it over the past 14 years. From the James Bond franchise to a teenage television dream based solely on their music, her voice has accompanied emotional wrecks across the expansive Western world—from audiences to executives alike. A constant within each of these released songs is her chameleon-like ability to weave narratives according to the visual world of the film or TV show. Whether it was in her solo albums or in the collaborations she has done on her own, she almost always pulls up to match the individual flair of musicians on almost every track.

After hearing "To Be Loved," a soulful Skyfall, Adele will inevitably appear in the minds of 007's fans around the world. Beyond Murray Gold and the Protomen's ba-jillionaires Howyn Prest, the TV take on DOCTOR WHO, Dead Again, Today's Special, etc., even though I may have only heard in Legion or Scary Movie 4, my first instinct is only to report Adele. It is my assumption that she is the only soundtrack singer who has had this disproportionately wide impact with only five songs across less than a dozen all-media.

If there are really more like them, and at this time, I am mistaken, please feel free to share more of this list from hell.

CHAPTER 15

Fashion and Beauty Influence

Adele is a complete force to be reckoned with in the fashion and beauty realms. With her signature cat-eye and wingtip, Adele has crafted her own signature style - and fans are absolutely in love. As expected, her work speaks for itself, and her songs continue to inspire significant fashion and beauty campaigns. Here, we're taking a look at some of the ways Adele influences the various industries, with a particular focus on fashion and makeup.

Adele has created an incredibly strong following over the years, and it makes perfect sense that fans would want to express their love for the singer in some kind of tangible way. One of the easiest ways to do so is through fashion. Adele has helped popularize many different types of fashion. When you think of the singer, you're likely to think of cozy, warm wool coats and beautiful gowns. It feels like she's been around forever, but it's only been relatively recently that Adele has grown in popularity - from her first American tour in 2011 and the release of her album "21" to where she is now. From the beginning, her style has reflected her music, and it's certainly only changed and matured since. Her style icon status didn't happen overnight, but gradually, her incredible voice and story helped put her on the map when it comes to fashion.

Her breakout hit single was "Chasing Pavements," and the song remains one of her best to date. It's truly no wonder that her deep and considerate lyrics have led to this type of association in one's mind, like an olfactory connection. It's an experience. Adele has, over the years, influenced and paved the way for a lot of other nostalgia-driven and retro-inspired artists, each reflecting a different era of music, from the soulful (like Amy Winehouse and Meghan Trainor) to alternative (like Lana Del Rey and Lorde). Fashion, in this sense, follows the same pattern.

Iconic Looks

Ever since her 2008 debut, Adele has been known for her soulful voice, catchy tunes, and vocal honesty. The songstress' beauty is just another thing about her that's made fans and the public alike fall in love with her. Apart from her incredible voice and piercing blue eyes, images of her iconic beauty look from the 'Someone Like You' video are seared into the pop culture landscape. Adele has continued to express herself through her fashion choices and beauty aesthetics in recent times. Her signature cat eyeliner, bold red lipstick, and expressive, perfectly groomed brows are said to have earned her her 'iconic' status.

Big, bouncy curls. Full, luscious lips. Sensationally sharp cat-eyes—Adele's got the works, as it were. These are the things that, together, have turned Adele into an icon. To focus on Adele today is to contemplate her Instagram presence, her philanthropy, her powerhouse voice, and her roles in television and film, and even where she comes from. It's also to recall the fact that, for about ten years running, she was the world's favorite guilded swan, an of-the-moment goal post for both personal and ageless beauty and the kind of old-school glamour that seemed long past and inaccessible to mere mortals. Her iconic smoky eye and perfect red lipstick combination is known and respected worldwide. No matter where Adele is, she always rocks perfectly groomed eyebrows and expressive eye makeup, typically matched with her red carpet looks. In recent times, the artist has continued to express herself through her iconic fashion choices in various ways and takes her aesthetic onto her nails, with various different dazzling designs that are always perfectly executed to match her iconic looks.

CHAPTER 16

Fan Community and Social Media

In the digital era, it goes without saying that the majority of pop stars have a significant following on social media platforms. When it comes to Adele, however, her performance on Facebook, Twitter, Instagram, and other platforms is not just good, but even noteworthy. People are listening carefully to what Adele shares about her private life, and the number of friends she now has is a key indicator of her social media success.

Adele's professional account on Facebook has over 62.5 million followers, and her official Twitter account has over 28.3 million followers. On Instagram since 2016, she has amassed 40.2 million followers. Rather than assuming these accounts just proclaim Adele's favorite events, they are possible to involve exclusive interviews, images from her recording sessions, and more.

"I in addition to my loyal follower group also have a chat with most of my distant friends, on Instagram it's mostly photographs of myself and my very loved ones," she chuckled. "So never grow to trust Instagram with accurate images of my life."

Adele's "fandom," according to Jenkins, has escalated massively since her 21 successes, increasing exponentially in her prominence due to her swift rise to acclaim. With the Instagram popularity follows, although there is no unique Instagram account just for her, more involvement is now within her grasp. Two popular Instagram accounts feature Adele because "Society from Adele" can be described as devoted to her fashion, with 453,000 followers and "The Adelephans". A combined 57,000 followers will allow Adele-movie-tribute highlighted in Adelekit to reach the mass shopper.

The followers of this 2, class according to the 'dreaded' Instagram version— account is categorized, the real chaser Adele include both suitors and epicures suggests the peak of her superstardom away from freedom. She has won 4,000 supporters on these collective sites. The Cube's fellow accountive, in proportion to their adherents, have 12,000-gridnaps and endman, signifying a probability of a 3—primary explanation, are unfold. Hosted for both 25 and 21 as enlist out of the 15 exclude the fellow accountive group.

Online Presence

Adele's online presence is characterized primarily by her absence. While she had profiles on social networks such as Twitter and Facebook, she could very rarely be seen professing her support to social causes, uploading photos taken at the studio or stage, tagging other celebrities, or discussing her songs and albums. Yet, one would assume that an artist of her stature would need to remain active on the social networks, communicating with her audience in a consistent manner.

Even if she was not a voice in her own social space, Adele's presence is discernible across Twitter accounts, Facebook pages, websites, and fan forums. When the singer released or promoted anything online – a photo, an album, a music video – fan activity on the digital spaces immediately rose. The promotion of an upload of any kind typically triggered all sorts of online conversations as fans and commentators shared links to content, discussed the artist's tweets or descriptions, and shared their analysis of 'conversations' that had ostensibly been initiated by Adele personally.

Much of the communication between Adele and her audience through the social network can be summarized as fan commentary, discussion of and support for Adele, and conversation with other fans. The conversations show the importance of audience-led communication on these networks, the function of the networks as a space for Adele's fans to express their affection, the energies that fans are willing to devote to "keeping up". Attention becomes a resource in itself. Attention towards a particular act gives that person or entity authority, influence, and in some cases performances such as minority or marginal representation. A type of social marketing capital is at work – those artists being plucked from obscurity and given the Right On Stamp of Approval via the repetition of tags and posts online.

CHAPTER 17

Concert Tours and Live Performances

One of the ways that Adele has been able to sell millions of albums and break records within short times is by taking advantage of the promotional strategy widely known as the concert tour. Smaller, more intimate performances by the singer include her use of live radio and television engagements. The major concert tours that the artist herself organizes have been coined "Adele Live" by news outlets and connected radio. When performing live, Adele represents an artist generation that may be loved most firstly and finally as a live performer.

Adele's performances are prized not only because of her warm personality, but also because of her fierce, brusque wit on stage. When she vocally shatters people by bursting into her powerful wails, her range engulfs the audience. The performances have been accused by some as being too melodramatic, but fewer still would deny that they can inspire young singers too. Adele's live shows are very nice to go to. A considerably less complement, but absolutely fitting for the artist, would be that Adele's infamously foul language and cheeky persona lead to humorous flubs, which have attracted Americans previously unfamiliar with her hits. Her fans are captivated, enamored, and obsessed by the emotional depths from whom her honey eyes reach all the way to the back of her enormous crowds, filling enormous venues that grow larger with every new release.

World Tours

Adele has done four global tours, starting with her An Evening with Adele tour in 2008 and following with the Adele: Live tour in 2009-2010; Adele Live in 2011-2012; and Adele Live 2016 in 2016-2017. Her latest concert tour, Adele Live, was the 15th highest-grossing tour of all time and was attended by 2 million fans. Each of her tour's tickets is one of the fastest-selling concert tickets, and her concert at the Royal Albert Hall sold out in just a whole 5 minutes.

Her concert tours have extensive influence and help Adele to reach a broad international audience. In 2016, on her first Australian tour, three tickets are sold every single second. The demand was so high that most of the tickets sold out within a few minutes. This is the first time that Adele has performed in Australia, and she is the only artist to sell out eight arena dates down under in one city in one big pop. Her second stop is held at Perth Stadium, and she will then sing her heart out at The Gabba (Brisbane), ANZ Stadium (Sydney), Adelaide Oval (Adelaide), Etihad Stadium (Melbourne), Domain Stadium (Perth) and the newly opened Optus Stadium in Perth, which is where the concert will be held. The Grammy award-winning singer will end her tour with four shows at Wembley Stadium in the UK. Her 2016-2017 tour saw her perform 122 shows in Europe, North America, Mexico, Australia and her native Britain. The London and Los Angeles shows will be filmed and feature in the production. The tour was well received by critics and audiences alike.

CHAPTER 18

Documentaries and Biographies

Fans of Adele's majestic vocals and infectious laugh have even more material to enjoy with so many documentaries and biographies in the works about the singer. Adele is allowing film cameras a rare, behind-the-scenes look into her life, characters' work on and off stage for a documentary to be released next fall. "Adele has been very private so far and she never spoke much about her wild years, her musical journey and subtle influences," a source told the paper. "But now she curates the show's content, there are likely to be insights into her relationships, her response to fame, and some of the most personal stories she wrote about."

Fans online compared their unique voices and music: Rodrigo released her debut album SOUR in 2021, and Adele is expected to release her upcoming album 30 on November 19. "Previous generations were inspired by their divas, as Britney Spears, were inspired by Madonna and others from their generation, in addition to an infinite number of pop stars in the following years...," one fan wrote. "But instead, Generation Z was influenced by people like Adele and now Olivia Rodrigo." During her 2015 tour, Adele will play a rare show at the legendary Los Angeles venue The Wiltern before squeezing into the 20,000-seat Staples Center in mid-summer. While Adele's global influence had never been surprising, the Wiltern Show became so special that NBC broadcast the song from the show after the Grammys. Later, Adele will be accompanied by Aretha Franklin and Beyoncé at the 2017 Women's March in Washington, D.C. to perform the "Sound of Music" hit "I".

Behind-the-Scenes Insights

Loyal fans will often love all things having to do with their music idols, meaning that they aren't just content experiencing an artist's discography. Instead, they will be interested in seeing those behind-the-scenes insights. Adele is one such artist that the public has great interest in. She has been in the business for just over a decade, but she has broken so many records and even set her own records. Besides, we have also been treated to authentic perspectives of the life and experiences of Adele, which have been painted in tracks and lyrics. Therefore, it is quite liberating to be able to see those very life experiences from the viewpoint of someone who truly lived them. Fortunately, there are documentaries and biographies available that can provide you with this behind-the-scenes perspective of Adele.

A lot of valuable insights can be gained from documentaries. If you find documentaries about Adele, then you may want to set aside the required time so you can watch. Moreover, it is a good idea to watch more than one documentary about Adele so you are able to gain a wholesome perspective on her life. If you're looking for some good Blu-ray concert films from Adele, then three options are available. The first option that is available, and in my opinion the one that you need to buy if you already have a Blu-ray player, is Adele: Live at Royal Albert Hall (2011).

CHAPTER 19

Future Projects and Collaborations

Adele has her sights set on numerous future projects. In September 2021, though without offering any details, she promised fans, "I'm going to be hanging a lot with you all from my streaming gift. I'm going to spend some time next year coming up with some of the most exciting things I can for you all to binge." There are also discussions of releasing a Christmas standard as a festive treat before she splits from her heartbreak ballads for singles from the new album. In 2022, fans can expect to see her at an increasing number of major music events, ticket availability for which will not be such a rare treat. She will take the David Geffen vocal coach on a cross-country voyage in Later... With Adele in order to participate in both the Oscars and the Brit Awards in March. It has also been noted that the Londoner is "much younger" and "she's changed." A full documentary is in the works in collaboration with her friend Oprah Winfrey, aptly named Adele One Night Only. It will give followers voice notes, unheard videos, and more glimpses behind-the-scenes. Sounds like an ideal project that is both gratifying and genuine!

She has yet to confirm the order in which the singles will be released from her upcoming record, nor has she provided definite release information. A few names have snuck their way into the public realm because she is having problems selecting the final collection. Her first record, "Honest," became the biggest selling in 2021 in the UK this week, bringing her to the top of the charts for the fourth week. Percentage Scaled to Sales, the album sold 37,000 copies last week and gave Adele an edge in the year's chart by about half a million copies. With 285,000 sales to date, "30" has become the fastest-selling album of 2021.

Upcoming Releases

Indeed, in the winter of 2021, just ahead of her appearance on Saturday Night Live, Adele announced the end of her upcoming album's secrecy and assured that it was on the way. With three public appearances and a Vogue interview, however, still no new music was available, despite the fact that the album, one of the most anticipated ones of the year, was complete and ready for release. In the meantime, an article about the possibility of Adele touring in March of 2022 for the first time since 2017 drew on Adele fan speculation about the dates of upcoming festival headlining announcements. What new projects are up on the horizon?

Further avenues for new lyrics dealing with her divorce from Simon Konecki remain, and a perfume line or others of the like could be equally likely as any other in light of Adele's already-existing partnership with her own charity and Mentos. The social media tabloids are almost regularly filled with audiences' fine/actory mess; increasing the number of live performances viewers could watch is one way to maintain nominal Adele hype. Wait. Are you serious? Adele says that she would not turn down a part if the right role for her came along in either an ensemble or single-starring film. There is growing suspicion that this may be the case after all. Adele doesn't get touched by as much sympathy as we seen to think. Major casting announcements ahead of premiering official trailers would not be wise— new music would drown out the dud of any new musical movie promises. The possibility in bridal and women's dress collections remains conspicuously lacking in hope. Another album would keep things exciting until 36 Roses are ninety percent sold.

CHAPTER 20

Conclusion

Adele's journey as an artist has spanned over ten years. No matter her age, Adele has released albums that have resonated with a broad spectrum of listeners. These albums follow Adele's personal and professional evolution as her music has matured and crossed into the pop genre. This case study has attempted to examine Adele and how she has become the artist she is today. Chapter one examined Richard Henriksen's 3-Dimensional model of music (voice, pitch, and beat) with the intention of understanding how Adele explains herself through music.

Chapter two examined the charts to understand how Adele's success was influenced by British cultural values of the noughties, as she could exist within and outside spaces of the commercial. Chapter three examined the 'exploitations' of Adele within this music she produces; her body; and in public speeches. It is an examination of the type of artist Adele is and the audiences she has the capacity to reach. Adele has a successful back catalog of music, but more than this, she has a successful 'story' that people like. Even if you do not like her music, Adele's media work convinces people that she is relatable and endearing. Adele is funny and charming in her interviews, she avoids the negativity and aggression that sales on irony, and thus she appeals to a demographic much wider than her music would suggest. Since the release of her first album 19, Adele has endeared herself to a market that crosses generations and spans genders. In the new generation who like her music, it is very possible fans are also taking inspiration from Adele, the woman, proving, as Ingham states, the importance of 'stories in helping us learn about the world,' including those 'constructed about lives in popular media and popular culture' (221). Adele is relatable for many people because she is a woman who has struggled but continued to succeed and continues to succeed. She has, in no uncertain terms, triumphed in adversity. For many, Adele represents the possibility of the American Dream, to go from "nothing" to something.

Key Takeaways and Reflections

As we reflect on all of the material provided throughout this unit, the following key takeaways begin to emerge. It is clear that Adele is a powerful, award-winning singer and songwriter with commercial and popular acclaim for her music. Not only was the theme of her musical catalogue of interest to both fans and listeners across generations, but the adversity she faced on a personal level piqued the curiosity and sympathy of the general public. The music and music videos of Adele exemplified her efforts to remain grounded and humble in the high stakes and over-the-top world of pop music. The various aspects of genteel, hardscrabble or hard work focusing on effort and immaculate skill without critique, in addition to exclusive ballgowns and championship wins, offer a peek at Adele and what she has to offer her fans and concertgoers that set her apart from the crowd. We are invited to hear this reflection in her music and then caught up in the desire to listen to such music, as well as to wallow and reminisce, drive to the shopping mall, put bubble bath in the drawn tub, and become the well-received rings in the fountain. Adele has sold more records and achieved more milestones in a year, but it is the soft, safe sound of sadness that keeps audiences coming back for more. This last section on who Adele is to a whole generation is the focus of our conclusion for this unit.

We are pleased to provide a brief summary of this project to you by identifying major milestones and accomplishments and the glimmers of insight that are generated throughout these materials. Adele can sing and is a songwriter with experience, plain and simple. She is self-fashioned as an audience everywoman. From stroke of success to stroke of misfortune, this Beatlesque powerhouse label became one of the top mainstream alternative bands. Her voice may be played by anyone as millions have been purchased as ringbacks or carry a photograph of Adele in their back pocket. Adele maintains that she is not motivated by a need to be known or glamorous and that she seeks to keep her private life private. After she determined herself as a big girl who wants to wear comfy maternity patterns on stage, she is continuously recognized as a no-frills kind of superstar.